Pavcula

Marie Curie

BRAVE SCIENTIST

Marie Curie

BRAVE SCIENTIST

by Keith Brandt
illustrated by Karen Milone

Troll Associates

Library of Congress Cataloging in Publication Data

Brandt, Keith (date)
    Marie Curie, brave scientist.

    Summary: A brief biography focusing on the youth of
the scientist who twice received the Nobel Prize for
her work with radium.
    1. Curie, Marie, 1867-1934—Juvenile literature.
2. Chemists—Poland—Biography—Juvenile literature.
[1. Curie, Marie, 1867-1934. 2. Chemists] I. Milone,
Karen, ill. II. Title.
QD22.C8B77 1983   530'.092'4 [B] [92]   82-16092
ISBN 0-89375-855-8
ISBN 0-89375-856-6 (pbk.)

10   9   8   7   6   5   4   3   2

Marie Curie

BRAVE SCIENTIST

The Sklodowski family did not have much money. They were not famous or very important. But these things did not matter to them. To the Sklodowski family of Warsaw, Poland, what *did* matter was education.

Mr. Sklodowski was a professor of mathematics and physics at a fine boys' school. Mrs. Sklodowska was the principal of a girls' school. (In Polish, the last names of males and females are spelled differently. The last names of men often end with an "i." The last names of women often end with an "a." That is why it was Mr. Sklodowski and Mrs. Sklodowska.)

The family lived at Mrs. Sklodowska's school, on Freta Street. So even before the children—the three girls, Zosia, Bronya, and Hela, and their brother, Joseph—started school themselves, school was a part of their lives. At dinner each night, they talked about school subjects. Mama might tell about a girl who wrote the most wonderful stories. Papa might tell about a boy who was way ahead of everyone else in mathematics. They both talked about books and writers and new ideas. And they always included their children in these talks.

This was the family into which a baby girl was born on November 7, 1867. Her name was Manya. She was a bubbly, bright-eyed little girl. Her brother and sisters fussed over her all the time. Manya was the pet of the family, and she loved this attention.

But Manya knew there was sadness in the house, too. Mrs. Sklodowska was very ill. She had tuberculosis, a disease of the lungs. In those days, there was no cure for this disease. The only

Zosia   Hela   Manya   Joseph   Bronya

treatment was rest. Sometimes the sick person got better. Most of the time, the patient got weaker and weaker, and finally died. Today, tuberculosis can be cured with penicillin and other medicines. But at that time, there was little hope.

When Mrs. Sklodowska came down with tuberculosis, she had to stop working. This meant the family was forced to move from their apartment. But then they had a bit of good luck. Mr. Sklodowski was offered an excellent job at another boys' high school. A large apartment came with this job. The family was sad to leave their old home, but they looked forward to a happy life in their new one. And everyone hoped that Mama's health would get better.

Mrs. Sklodowska could not be with her children very much. She was afraid that they would catch her disease. So she did not hug or kiss them or hold any of them on her lap. The older children understood the reason for this. But Manya didn't. She only knew that hugs and kisses came from Papa and her brother and sisters. Mama had a sweet, loving smile, and would stroke Manya's head softly. But never once did she kiss the child.

In many ways, big sister Zosia took Mama's place with Manya. The little girl waited for Zosia to come home from school every afternoon. Then they would go for a walk to the candy shop down the street. Zosia told stories to Manya, sang songs to her, and played all kinds of games with her. Manya was a very bright girl. Once she

heard a story, she never forgot it. Weeks after, she could repeat it exactly as Zosia had told it.

Manya's amazing memory worked this way all the time. She remembered every conversation she ever heard. She remembered every fact she learned. If she was told to do something she didn't want to do, and if she didn't do it, she could not get away with saying, "Oh, I forgot."

Manya tried this excuse once or twice, but Papa just smiled and said, "Come, come, little one. You, who remember what I said to Mama at dinner three weeks ago! You did not *forget* to put away your toys. Now, did you?"

Manya giggled and hid her face behind her hands. She knew Papa wasn't angry, and that he would not punish her. Mr. Sklodowski did not like to punish his children, even when they misbehaved. They were never spanked or yelled at. Instead, Mr. Sklodowski would talk quietly to them. He treated his children as if they were grownups who should be respected. And they tried to behave that way.

13

When Manya was four years old, she showed just how bright she was. Seven-year-old Bronya was learning to read. One day, when she got tired of studying by herself, Bronya decided to play teacher with Manya. Bronya cut pieces of cardboard into the shapes of the letters of the alphabet. She stood them against a wall and pointed at them, one by one, with a ruler. And she said each letter aloud.

"Now, Manya," she said in a teacher's voice, "come to the front of the room. Please point to the letter *d*."

Manya was sitting cross-legged on the floor.

She got up, went to the wall, and pointed at the
d. Then she curtsied.

"Very good, Manya," her sister said. "Now,
please show me the s."

Manya did this, too. And all the other letters
of the alphabet. "Next," Bronya said, "we will
study how to spell words."

Bronya could not spell very many words
herself. Even so, the two little girls put together
words with their cut-out letters. Some of them
were real words, and some of them were not. But
it didn't matter to the girls. The spelling game
was so much fun that they played it every day
for weeks.

Then, one day, Bronya was reading out loud
for Mama and Papa. She read very slowly,
working hard to say every word. Manya was
sitting on the arm of Papa's chair, listening.
Then she began to fidget. At last, she sighed,
stood up, and took the book out of Bronya's
hands. And she began to read to them, easily and
without a mistake.

Mr. and Mrs. Sklodowski were stunned! Bronya's face turned red with anger. She snatched the book from Manya's hands and ran from the room. Manya started to cry. "I'm sorry!" she sobbed. "I didn't do it on purpose. It's not my fault—it's not Bronya's fault! It's only because it was so easy!" The four-year-old child did not understand the looks on her parents' faces. Manya thought they were angry, but they were only extremely surprised that she could read.

Manya's parents were very pleased that she was so bright. But they felt there was time enough for reading when Manya went to school. Then she would have to study a lot. Now, the little girl should run and play.

And Manya liked to play, especially with the wooden blocks their uncle had given them for Christmas. "Here," he said, "now you can build castles and houses and bridges."

At first, the children used the blocks that way. Then they found a better game to play. War! Joseph and Hela were one team, Bronya and Manya were the other. Each team would build a fort and open fire. Blocks would fly back and forth across the playroom, until both forts were knocked down. It was great fun, and Manya remembered those wild battles for the rest of her life.

She also remembered many wonderful vacations in the country. Every summer, when school let out, the family left Warsaw. The Sklodowskis could not afford to go to a summer resort. But they had many relations living in the country who welcomed them each year. Manya loved running barefoot through the grassy fields, climbing trees, wading in the streams, and eating cherries and apples she picked herself.

For many people, however, life in Poland was not happy. The country was not free. Russia ruled Poland strictly. Polish schoolchildren had to learn their lessons in Russian. And they were forbidden to speak their own language in school.

When the Russians said Polish children should not be taught much science, Mr. Sklodowski was sad. He took his scientific equipment—scales, minerals, and test tubes—and put them in a glass case in his study.

Manya liked to look in the glass case. She thought the shelves held the most beautiful things she had ever seen. "Papa, what do you call these pretty, shiny things?" she asked one day.

"That is phy-sics ap-pa-ra-tus," he answered.

The words sounded lovely to Manya's ears. And she wanted to learn how to use those magical things. *Some day,* she told herself, *I will have phy-sics ap-pa-ra-tus of my own.* Of course, the five-year-old did not know what the words "physics apparatus" meant. She only knew she wouldn't rest until she understood everything about them.

Manya had glorious dreams for the future. But right now, the family had many problems. In September of 1873, when Manya was almost six years old, the family returned to Warsaw from the country. They were met by bad news—a letter from the school principal. It said that Mr. Sklodowski's job was being made less important, and that his salary was being cut. Finally, the family was ordered to move out of their apartment at the school.

The seven Sklodowskis moved to a smaller apartment. Even then, there wasn't enough money for their needs. To earn more money, they took in ten of Mr. Sklodowski's students to board with them.

The bedrooms were filled with boarders, and the Sklodowski children slept on couches and cots in the dining room. The children had to be up early every morning, to put away the bedding and set the table for the boarders' breakfast. There was no privacy, and the best food had to go to the people who paid the rent.

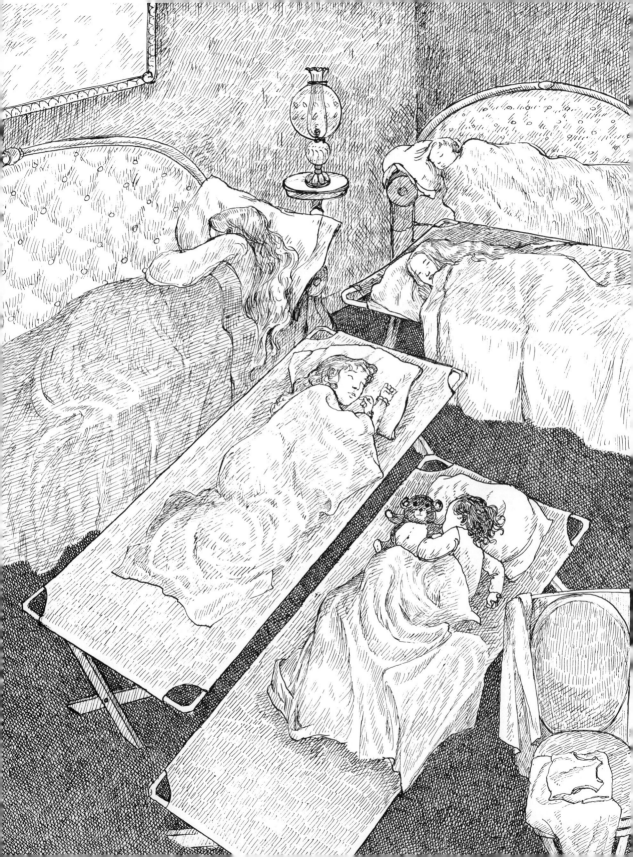

It wasn't easy for the Sklodowskis. Papa felt like a failure. As sick as she was, Mama tried to help. She taught herself to make shoes. It was hard work—cutting out the leather shapes, then sewing them into shoes with a heavy needle and thread. But it was a lot less expensive than buying shoes in a store.

Mrs. Sklodowska's health was failing. The doctor said she must go to a warm, sunny place for a long rest. The family hoped this would cure her tuberculosis. Even though it meant using the last of the family's savings, Mrs. Sklodowska and Zosia went to the south of France.

They came home a year later. Manya rushed to welcome them. Manya prayed that her mother would be well enough to scoop up her little girl and kiss her for the very first time! But it was not to be. Mrs. Sklodowska was thin and very weak. She was even sicker than when she had left for France.

In January 1876, when Manya was eight years old, more sickness came to the Sklodowski home. One of the boarders fell ill with typhus, a very serious disease. Bronya and Zosia caught it from him. After weeks of very high fever, Bronya began to recover. But fourteen-year-old Zosia died. It came as a terrible blow to Manya. Zosia, who had been like a mother to her, was gone. And the sadness did not end with that. Mrs. Sklodowska's condition was growing worse.

Finally, on May 9, 1878, she died.

Every time Manya thought of Mama and Zosia, she felt so lonely. She found that the only way she could escape from her sorrow was to bury herself in a book. Manya read everything she could get her hands on—poetry, textbooks, novels, and scientific journals from her father's library. She read books written in Polish, Russian, French, and German. And she remembered every word she read. The harder the book was, the more she liked it.

Manya had another talent as unusual as her memory. She could shut out all the sounds around her when she was reading. People would talk to her, even call her name, but she heard nothing. All the Sklodowski children and the many boarders studied at the dining-room table at the same time. So there was always a lot of noise. But Manya sat in her chair and read on, as if floating in a sea of silence.

All of the children laughed at how Manya was deaf to everything when she was reading. One day they cooked up an idea. They put a chair on each side of hers. Then they put another chair behind her. Next, they stacked two more chairs on top of the first three. Finally, they laid a chair on top of all of them. Now, Manya was surrounded by a pyramid of six chairs.

Not once did Manya look up from her book. Through all the giggling and building, she kept on reading. For half an hour, the children watched and waited. The tension grew. Then, at last, Manya closed her book and started to get up. As she pushed back her chair, the pyramid came crashing down. Chairs tumbled left and right. The mischief-makers howled with laughter.

Manya didn't laugh—she was startled. She stood still for a moment, watching Hela and Bronya rolling on the floor, giggling madly. Then Manya angrily picked up her book and walked out of the room.

Even though she didn't find it funny at the time, Manya remembered the pyramid of chairs for as long as she lived. Years later, when she was grown, she was still able to blot out all the sounds around her. This ability to keep her mind locked on what she was doing helped her to become one of the world's greatest scientists. Sometimes co-workers in her laboratory complained when they could not get her attention. Then she would laugh and tell them the joke of the "pyramid of chairs." She would finish the story by saying that a room could blow up under her feet, and she would not know it, if she was working when it happened.

As a child, Manya's love of reading and her great memory made her a prize pupil. At Mademoiselle Sikorska's school for girls, as at all Polish schools, classes were supposed to be taught in Russian. But the Poles refused to give up their own language. In secret, they held classes in Polish history, which were taught in Polish. But, of course, they could not let the Russian school inspectors know what they were doing.

There was a special bell signal to let everyone know when an inspector entered Manya's school. When this signal sounded, the Polish books disappeared. And any time the inspector came into Manya's classroom, the teacher called on her to recite.

Manya was the picture of the perfect pupil. She stood straight, her face calm and serious. Her hair was neatly braided and tied with a dark ribbon. She wore the school uniform: a navy-blue wool dress with steel buttons and a starched white collar. On her feet were dark stockings and polished, black, high-laced shoes.

Using her faultless memory and speaking perfect Russian, Manya repeated page after page of the Russian history book. She always pleased the inspector. But she hated everything about his visit. She loved her country and her language. It was painful for her to make believe that she was a faithful subject of the Russian rulers. When the inspector was gone, she cried. Not even the praise of her classmates could take away the shame she felt at having to play this terrible game.

Manya graduated from Mademoiselle Sikorska's school at the top of her class. Then she became a

student at the best girls' high school in Warsaw. It was called the *gymnasium*. In Europe, a gymnasium is not a place to play sports. It is a high school attended by only the brightest students.

Manya plunged into her studies with joy. Math and science were her favorite subjects, but she did well in everything. And every year she won top honors. When she graduated, on June 12, 1883, the fifteen-year-old girl was awarded a gold medal. It was the highest prize a student could get.

Now, Manya wanted to go to college. There, she could really explore the world of science. That was what she wanted to do with her life. But women were not allowed to go to college in Poland. Manya was furious. It was like being told to lock her mind in a small room and keep it there forever.

Manya lost all interest in everything around her. She didn't want to eat. She sat staring out a window for hours. She cried when her family tried to cheer her up. At last, her father sent her to stay with relations in the country. He hoped that

the rest would lift her out of her gloom.

At first, it didn't seem to help. But, at last, the fun and beauty of country living began to work on her. As she wrote to her best friend, Kazia, "There is plenty of water for swimming and boating, which delights me. I am learning to row—I am getting on quite well—and the bathing is ideal. We do everything that comes into our heads, we sleep sometimes at night and sometimes by day. We dance, and we do so many crazy things that sometimes we deserve to be locked up!"

When Manya returned to her home in Warsaw, she felt a lot better. She had a plan now. She would work and save her money. Then, when she had enough, she would go to France and study science at the Sorbonne University.

During the day, she gave lessons to young children. At night, she attended the "floating university." This was a group of people who met in secret. Some were women who were not allowed to go to college. Some were men who could not afford to go to college. And the teachers were Polish patriots who did not want their people to be ignorant.

At the floating university, Manya studied anatomy, natural history, chemistry, biology, mathematics, and literature. She also found time to teach literature and Polish history to working women. This was the only way these women would ever get any education.

When Manya turned eighteen, she and Bronya thought up a new plan. Bronya also wanted to go to college. She wished to become a doctor. So the sisters agreed to help each other. Bronya would take their savings and begin studying at the Sorbonne in Paris. Manya would get a job as a governess and send her earnings to Bronya. Then, when Bronya became a doctor, she would bring Manya to Paris and pay *her* way through school.

For the next six years, Manya worked as a governess, while her sister finished medical school. Then, Bronya sent for Manya. And on November 3, 1891, Manya enrolled at the Sorbonne, as Marie Sklodowska. It was the first step on a path that would lead to greatness.

As a student, Marie lived in an almost bare room in an attic near the school. She spent next to nothing on rent and food. Just about every bit of money went for school and books. And every moment was spent studying or attending classes.

It was far from easy, even for Marie. The classes were taught in French, and this was still a difficult language for her. Also, her French classmates were way ahead of her in their scientific education.

But Marie's heart and mind were set on one goal—a life dedicated to science. No obstacle was too great for her to overcome. And sure enough, in 1893, she received an advanced degree in physics—and was first in her class! And one year later, Marie received an advanced degree in mathematics. This time she was second in her class.

Marie's education still wasn't finished. She continued to study at the Sorbonne and to do laboratory research on an element called uranium. Not long before this, scientists had discovered that uranium gave off unexplained rays. We now know that these rays are atomic radiation. But it was a total mystery in the 1890s. Marie set out to solve that mystery.

About this time, Marie met Pierre Curie, a professor of physics at the Sorbonne. Their interest in science brought them together, and their friendship soon turned to love. They were married on July 26, 1895. With her husband's help and advice, Marie Curie continued her research in radioactivity. And in 1898, Marie and Pierre discovered two elements. They named them polonium and radium. For this great work, the Curies were awarded the Nobel Prize for Physics in 1903. Marie Curie had become the first woman to receive the Nobel Prize.

Then, in 1906, tragedy again came into Marie's life. Pierre was struck and killed by a horse-drawn wagon. And, once again, she buried herself in work, at the same time raising two young daughters, Irene and Eve.

Marie continued to work with radium until, at last, she found a way to make it pure. This form of radium was—and is—used to treat cancer patients. For this work, Marie Curie was awarded the Nobel Prize for Chemistry in 1911. It was the first time anyone had ever won two Nobel Prizes!

Though she became world famous, Marie Curie wanted to be nothing more than a scientist and mother. Until she died, on July 4, 1934, she continued to work in her beloved laboratory. She did not care about glory or money. Only science and what it could do for people were truly important to the great Madame Curie. The little girl who had seen such beauty in her father's "phy-sics ap-pa-ra-tus" had grown into one of the world's greatest scientists.